FRED BASSET

by Alex Graham

Chapmans Publishers Ltd
141-143 Drury Lane
London WC2B 5TB

First Published by Chapmans 1991

© Associated Newspapers plc 1991

ISBN 1 85592 717 9

Printed and bound in Great Britain by
William Clowes Ltd. Beccles and London

That's the high frequency whistle that dogs can hear and humans can't
But if I ignore it and he can't hear it he won't know if it's working or not, will he?
So I'll ignore it, he'll think it isn't working, and I'll join him when I'm ready
8578
ALEX GRAHAM
© Associated Newspapers Ltd., 1991

I'M OFF TO THE GOLF CLUB
Please can I come?
NO, YOU CAN'T, FRED, IT'S A COMPETITION. NO DOGS ALLOWED
Pity!
See? I understand every word he says, and he can read my thoughts
8579
ALEX GRAHAM
© Associated Newspapers Ltd., 1991

He looks familiar... who can it be?
8489
Off duty and out of uniform, I didn't recognise him! IT'S THE POSTMAN!
© Associated Newspapers Ltd., 1991
And I let him pass unscathed!
ALEX GRAHAM

FETCH!
We work on the reward system
8490.
He throws the ball, I retrieve it...
© Associated Newspapers Ltd., 1991
GOOD BOY!
...and I reward him by wagging my tail!
ALEX GRAHAM

© Associated Newspapers Ltd., 1991
The things that go on in this neighbourhood.... There was that riotous all-night party at Number 12
...And the night the police were called in to the Smith home....Everybody knows about the young lady in Number 27...
...And there are rumours about the foreign gentleman who recently bought Number 18.... Believe me, if I could talk I'd have a few stories to tell
ALEX GRAHAM
8540

Carrying the tea-tray she stumbled, and everything fell to the floor. He jumped up to help, and crashed into the standard lamp, which fell on to the television
This blew the main fuse, and all the lights went out! Nobody hurt, thank goodness!
In the resulting confusion I got away with a buttered scone
© Associated Newspapers Ltd., 1991
ALEX GRAHAM
8541

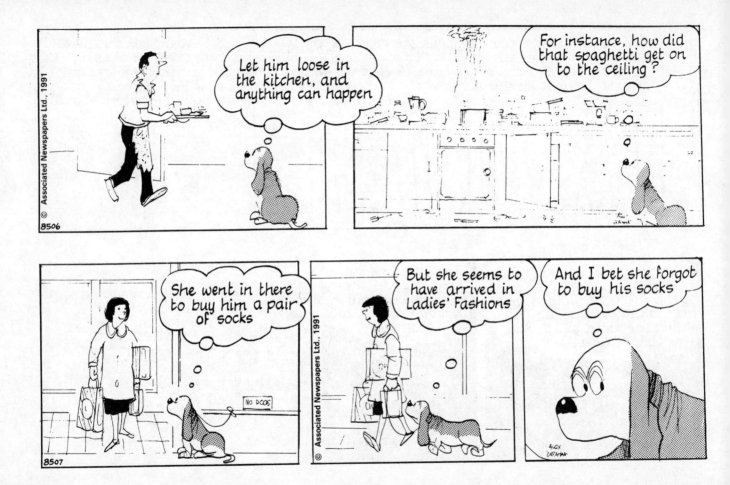

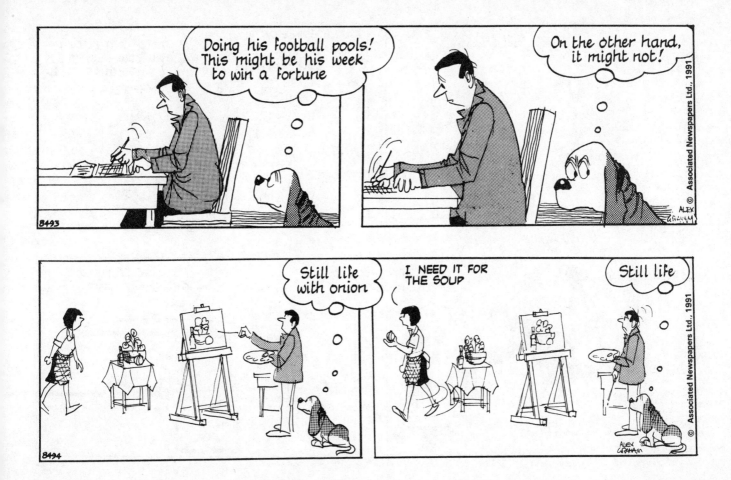

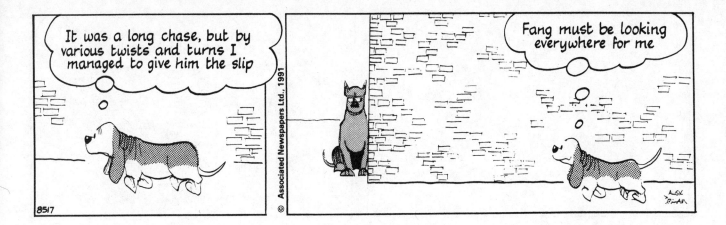

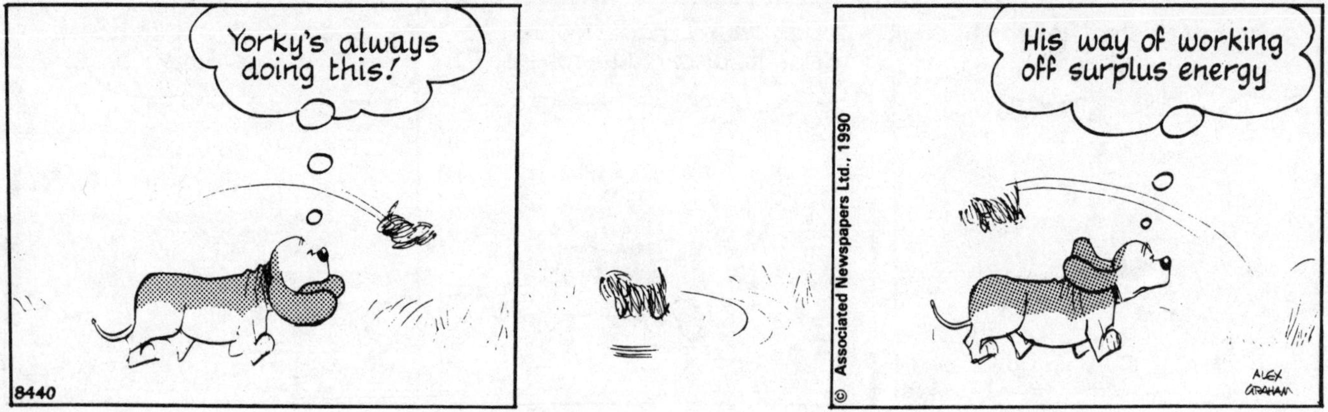
Yorky's always doing this!
His way of working off surplus energy
8440
© Associated Newspapers Ltd., 1990
ALEX GRAHAM

FRED!
Sorry! I am unable to answer your call
At the moment I am engaged
Please try again later
8566
ALEX GRAHAM
© Associated Newspapers Ltd., 1991